English to Ukranian

Bilingual Learning Made Fun and
Easy with Words and Pictures

by Sharon Purtill

Books

Книги

Мої перші слова

англійською та українською мовою

My First Words
A - Z
English to Ukrainian

Bilingual Learning Made Fun and
Easy with Words and Pictures

by Sharon Purtill

Published by Dunhill Clare Publishing - Ontario, Canada

dunhillclare@gmail.com

Paperback edition ISBN: 978-1-990469-17-6
Digital edition ISBN: 978-1-990469-18-3

Library and Archives Canada Cataloguing in Publications

Apple

Яблуко

(Yabluko)

Books

Книги

(Knyhy)

Cat

KIT

(Kit)

Dog

Собака

(Sobaka)

Elephant

Слон

(Slon)

Flower

Квітка
(Kvitka)

Giraffe

Жираф

(Zhyraf)

Hat

Капелюх

(Kapeliukh)

Ice Cream

Морозиво

(Morozyvo)

Jacket

Піджак

(Pidzhak)

Keys

Ключі

(Kliuchi)

Leaf

Лист
(**Lyst**)

Milk

Молоко
(Moloko)

Nest

Гніздо
(Hnizdo)

Orange

Апельсин

(Apelsyn)

Pot

Кастрюля
(**Kastriulia**)

Quilt

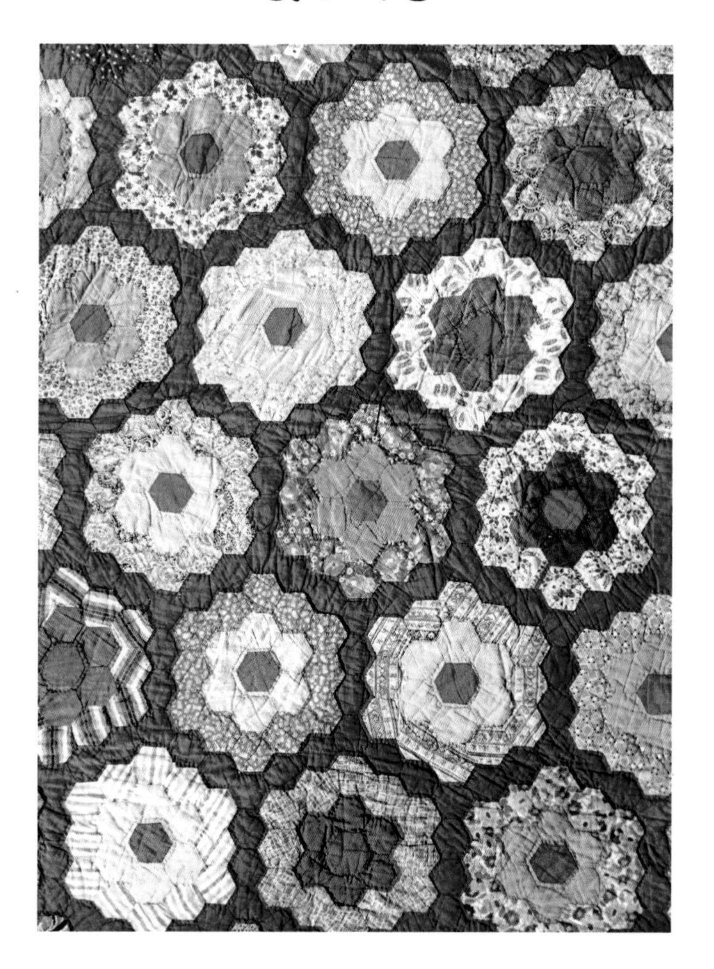

Ковдра

(Kovdra)

Rabbit

Кролик

(Krolyk)

Shoe

Взуття

(Vzuttia)

Table

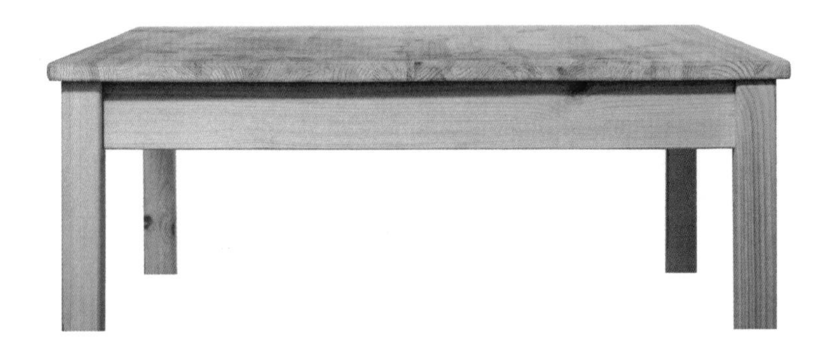

Стіл

(Stil)

Umbrella

Парасолька

(Parasol'ka)

Vacuum Cleaner

Пилосос

(Pylosos)

Watermelon

Кавун

(Kavun)

Xylophone

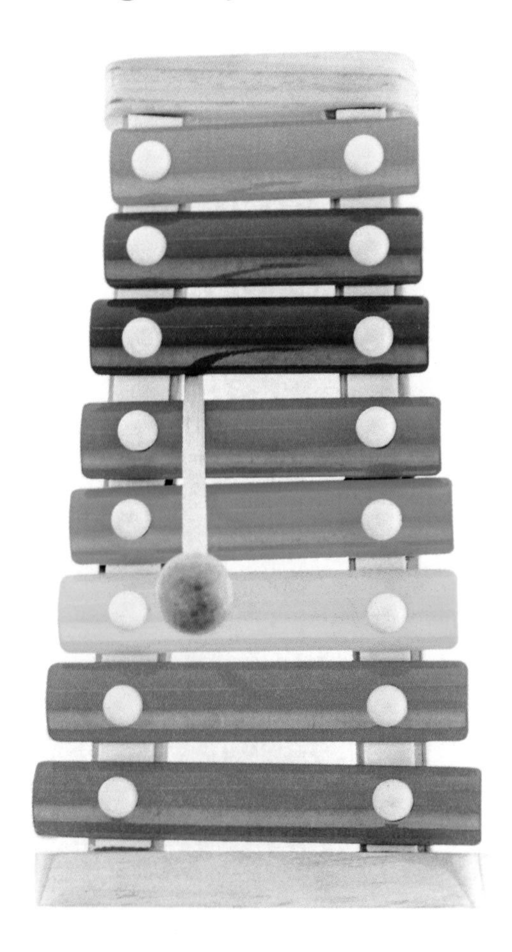

Ксилофон

(ksylofon)

Yellow

Жовтий

(zhovtyi)

Zebra

Зебра
(Zebra)

Bonus Words

English and Ukrainian

Let's learn common words for items
found in and around the home.

Can Be Found In The Kitchen

Можна знайти на кухні

(Mozhna znaity na kukhni)

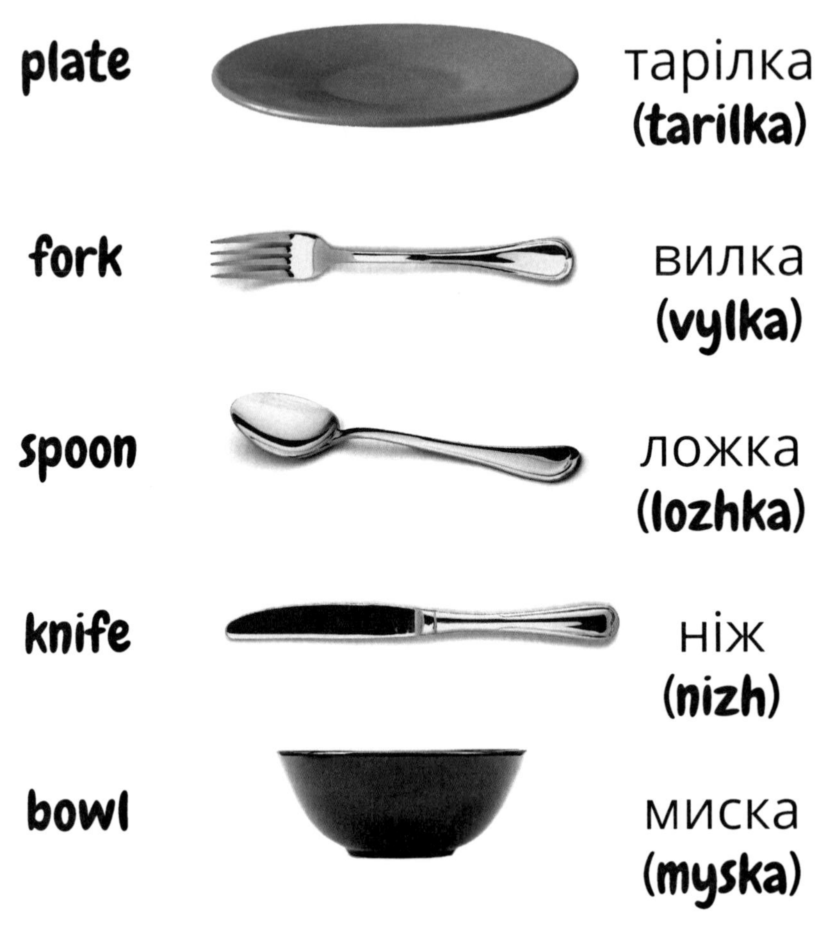

plate — тарілка **(tarilka)**

fork — вилка **(vylka)**

spoon — ложка **(lozhka)**

knife — ніж **(nizh)**

bowl — миска **(myska)**

plastic cup — пластиковий стаканчик **(plastykovyi stakanchyk**

Can Be Found In The Bathroom
Можна знайти у ванній
(Mozhna znaity u vannii)

toothpaste

зубна паста
(zubna pasta)

toothbrush

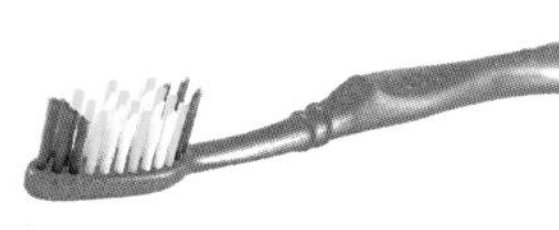

зубна щітка
(zubna shchitka)

hair brush

щітка для волосся
(shchitka dlya volossya)

comb

гребінець
(hrebinets')

towel

рушник
(rushnyk)

Can Be Found In The Bedroom
Можна знайти в спальні
(Mozhna znaity v spal'ni)

bed

ліжко
(lizhko)

blankets

ковдри
(kovdry)

pillow

подушка
(podushka)

dresser

комод
(komod)

toys

іграшки
(ihrashky)

Can Be Found In The Living Room
Можна знайти у вітальні
(Mozhna znaity u vital'ni)

television 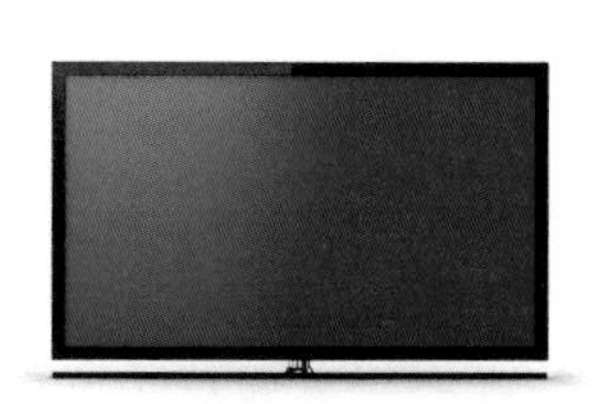 телевізор **(televizor)**

chair  крісло **(krislo)**

rug  килимок **(kylymok)**

lamp  лампа **(lampa)**

couch  диван **(dyvan)**

Can Be Found Outside
Можна знайти зовні
(Mozhna znaity zovni)

tree — дерево **(derevo)**

car  автівка **(avtivka)**

truck  вантажівка **(vantazhivka)**

bike  велосипед **(velosyped)**

grass  трава **(trava)**